EGYPT

A *terra magica* BOOK

EGYPT

PHOTOGRAPHS BY HED WIMMER AND OTHERS

TEXT BY PETER P. RIESTERER

LAYOUT BY HANNS REICH

HILL AND WANG · NEW YORK

Published in the United States of America by Hill and Wang, Inc., 1964. Library of Congress catalog card number: 64-15378. © 1963 Hanns Reich Verlag, Munich. All rights reserved, including those of photographic reproduction, reprint in whole or in part, and diffusion by radio and television. Printed in Switzerland.

LAND
AND
PEOPLE

They who built in granite, they who hewed a chamber into the pyramid, they who added beauty to this beautiful work . . . their altars are as empty as are the altars of those who die, tired and unmourned, upon the riverbank.
(Old Egyptian proverb)

When Herodotus (*c.* 484-425 B.C.), the first historian, traveled through Egypt, Athenians and rebellious Egyptians were engaged in a losing war against the Persians in the land along the Nile. But the land itself still had all the unspoiled charm we know from the stories in the Bible. Lotus flowers blossomed beside still waters and thickets of papyrus covered vast areas along the Nile; crocodiles basked on the sand bars.

Herodotus saw the pyramids. He discovered, in one of the limestone facings, a businesslike inscription that showed how many radishes, onions, and cloves of garlic had been disbursed to the workmen who had labored at the construction of that gigantic stone monument for forty years. He observed the gradual extinction of the old customs and traditions; he saw the delta swamplands where bird-catchers had their dwellings. Sun temples and sanctuaries awed him as they awe the modern tourist who sees those tremendous memorials for the first time. He also saw the great, mysterious miracle of the annual flooding of the Nile which transforms the regions along the river into fertile farmland; and he coined the apt, still valid phrase: "Egypt is a gift of the Nile."

A journey through Egypt today is a journey into the past. The narrow strips on either side of the Nile, from Cairo to Aswân, have become one vast, difficult-to-survey outdoor museum of temples, pyramids, rock carvings, and tombs, framed by verdant palm groves, deserts, and fields. Lazily the river flows north, its water now green-blue, now coffee brown; only during flood time – when, in our own regions, summer fades into early autumn – does the river turn into a raging torrent and overflow its banks, sometimes carrying away houses, people, and cattle.

The tourist who visits Egypt today usually arrives by airplane in Cairo, the Egyptian *Masr-el-Kahira* (population roughly 2,500,000), the biggest city in Africa and, at the same time, the most important center of trade with Europe and Asia. In the distance he sees the slim towers of minarets and the domes of mosques outlined against the sky, and suddenly feels the proximity of Oriental life. But this impression soon fades, when he rides through the streets of the capital: beautiful parks flank the road, flowering gardens surround the residential sections; in the center of the city his eye is drawn to many-storied modern office buildings among palm trees, tamarisks, and sycamores. Gone are the charcoal braziers that once graced every hotel lobby. There is central heating now and, in summer, air conditioning. Shops and store windows display merchandise from the United States, Germany, France, Switzerland; lumbering trucks and noisy buses dominate traffic. The city is a growing metropolis.

When the tourist has had enough of this American-style hustle and bustle, he need only walk a few blocks south and plunge into the Old City. It lies at the foot of the citadel whose walls are partly constructed of stones from the pyramids. He can wander through the silent mosque of Mehemet Ali, called the "Alabaster Mosque" by the guide; or, he can visit "Joseph's Fountain" to the southeast. Legend has it that this is where the Biblical Joseph was imprisoned. He can visit the elaborately ornamented mosque of Sultan Hasan, the most important example of Arab architecture in Egypt; or he can walk to the mosque of Al Azhar, "The Blossoming," where students of the Islamic University study in great halls and courtyards. Nearby are old Arab residences: the master's chambers are laid out around a courtyard; upper rooms contain the harem and rooms for women, children, and slaves. Just a few steps further on, there is typical Oriental activity; the bazaar quarters of Muski and Khan el Khalil, where rugs, brocades, copperware, gold, and silver are on display and where the gullible tourist can buy all sorts of faked antiquities. From Cairo the traveler can drive along a desert road to Alexandria, and there, where the desert stretches toward the sky, he might see mirages.

In the city of Alexander the Great, art lovers will discover that what they have come to see exists only in the museums. Alexandria itself is a Mediterranean resort, a bathing beach where, at dusk, rich Egyptians stroll through the gardens of the deposed King Farouk. And outside that city are delight after delight, in the salt flats and wide regions where fertile farmland is wrested from stagnant lakes and sandy desert. Here and there are water wheels like those that were used in Pharaoh's time; and all around, men and women till the soil. There are also great vegetable plantations and orchards, brand-new co-operative settlements, groves of date palms. Interspersed with patches of desert, the region stretches eastward as far as the Suez Canal.

On the other hand, the tourist might turn southwest from Cairo and travel past the pyramids to the Faiyûm Oasis where, as early as the nineteenth century B.C., a canal led from the Nile to the big depression in the ground, forming an artificial lake against the "seven lean years." Fat black water buffaloes lie lazy in the swamps and canals, and ancient water scoops and water wheels make the tourist feel that he has traveled back for thousands of years. Brilliantly colored birds flit across the water. For the big lake still exists, though neither lotus nor papyrus grows on its shores. Those plants, whose images we find in almost every Egyptian tomb, do not grow wild in Egypt any more.

Looking toward the western desert lands at night, our traveler will see isolated dots of light hovering above a plateau. Those are the electrically illuminated pyramids and the ancient Sphinx, whose nose was shot off by Mameluke cannon balls in the time of Napoleon. Besieged by tourists all day, the Sphinx does not even rest at night.

A railroad travels up the Nile as far as Aswân. Colorful scenes repeat themselves: cotton and rice fields, doom palms, tobacco plantations, clover, wheat, banana groves. In between, white buildings, turret-shaped structures like fairy-tale palaces, with pigeons fluttering around them. These are the pigeon coves of the fellahin, who fertilize their fields with the precious pigeon droppings.

At some points the fertile land narrows to a mere strip, at others it expands for miles to the east and west. Near Beni Hasan are the first rock tombs, caves hewn into the stone and decorated with marvelous wall paintings that depict rare birds and other creatures. These caves date back to the Middle Kingdom (c. 2040-1650 B.C.) and are now much faded and damaged. The same period, during which all private property was confiscated and returned to the state, also produced barbaric, clumsy statues.

After a journey of hundreds of miles the valley suddenly opens out and from the brown-green landscape rise the columns and portals of Karnak and Luxor. From here the princes of the XVIIth dynasty (c. 1550 B.C.) led the struggle against the foreign Hyksos who ruled Egypt for some time.

The kings of the XVIIIth dynasty (c. 1550-1300 B.C.) and the rulers who succeeded them built halls and houses for their gods, mysterious sanctuaries, at Thebes, the Luxor of today. The kings themselves were buried on the western bank of the river. They transformed the desert into a flower garden. Hatshepsut, a queen of this dynasty, the first woman to send a fleet to the legendary land of Punt, had a temple built for herself on the western bank and surrounded it with a lake planted with incense trees that had to be specially brought from Punt and with sycamores: "The little sycamore she has planted with her own hand begins to speak. The rustling of its leaves is as sweet as the scent of honey. It is beautiful; its graceful fresh boughs are laden with ripe fruit redder than the fruit of the jasper . . .," an inscription says.

The ancient Greeks were drawn to Luxor, which they called "Thebes of the Hundred Doors." But in our own era, Thebes did not attract art lovers and tourists until Lord Carnarvon and Howard Carter discovered the Valley of the Kings in 1922 to 1923. Carter excavated the tomb of Tutankhamen (XVIIIth dynasty), which was only slightly damaged. All the other burial sites had long been opened, plundered, and robbed in the days of the Pharaohs. The sarcophagi had been broken open, the objects found in the graves sold on the sly. There exists the confession of eight thieves who broke into the grave of Shepseskaf around 1100 B.C.:

"Then we opened the sarcophagi and the bands in which they rested. We found the venerable mummy of that king . . . with many golden amulets and much jewelry around its neck. The head was covered with gold. The venerable mummy of this king was completely covered with gold leaf and his sarcophagus was plated with gold inside and out and set about with splendid jewels. We tore off the gold which we had found on this god's venerable mummy, and also his amulets and jewels that hung upon his neck, and the bands that held them. We found the royal wife ornamented in the same way, and we tore away everything we found on her. We burned her bands and also stole her household goods, the vessels of gold and silver. Then we divided the gold we had found upon this god, upon the mummies, the amulets, jewelry, and bands, into eight parts."

Such works of art and precious objects as have come down to us from that distant period are still being found here and there in the country and are kept behind glass in the museum in Cairo. But even there they have not always been safe. Whole collections are missing from the inventory; the heaviest and most valuable ceremonial staff was stolen right out of the glass case that contains Tutankhamen's gold mask.

From Luxor, white sailboats carry the tourist to the opposite shore, where the Valley of the Kings lies: a desert landscape with hot winds and cool burial chambers whose walls are covered with texts from the Book of the Dead. White sails keep taking tourists back and forth across the river. Deeply tanned men at the tillers sing, as in the days of old, "Hela, hela, we pray to the Prophet. To the Nile, who heals the sick. To Allah, who makes our work easy. O great Ferryman, lead us home. Hela, hela."

South of Luxor, there are extensive sugar-cane fields. Bananas grow on some islands in the Nile. To the east, the gray Arabian Desert creeps close to the Nile and behind it

8

red mountains, gleaming in the sun, reach to the sea. In the days of antiquity a great road led through this region, connecting the big water with the gold mines of Egypt.

On the way to Aswân a few villages stand solitary among the rocks. It is an arid land where men live a primitive life: the precious water with which they quench their thirst and irrigate their cucumber fields has to be fetched from the Nile. Toward the west the desert, pale yellow near Luxor, turns reddish gold. Here begins the region of the great cataracts of the Nile around Aswân.

Aswân today is a splendid summer resort. Outside the city gates where foreigners seldom go, where no dragoman (tourist guide) will take you, the Bisharin still dwell in tent-like houses. A proud people in blue and red garments, they call themselves the rightful descendants of the ancient Egyptians. Their eyes are fierce, their hair is wild.

The city itself appears rather European at first sight, with just a breath of the Orient. But as the tourist penetrates further, he encounters marvel upon marvel. The streets are draped with awnings against the hot sun, under which merchants, hagglers, laborers, and witch doctors meet. Sweetmeats are sold from little movable carts lighted by candles. In one corner, an old man roasts almonds on a little stove. He praises the delicacies he has to sell in a sleepy singsong. Crisp bread is baking in wooden ovens. Right next door, men lie on their knees and pray to God in a niche of the mosque. Veiled women creep through the narrow streets and pull their headcloths lower over their faces when they meet the curious stare of a stranger. In a little square that smells of Turkish coffee, young people are having a kind of party. There is a juggler, a fire-eater, and a card player whose tricks entertain the youthful audience.

Hundreds of green islands float on the Nile near Aswân. Sailboats cruise from isle to isle and to a larger, flower-decked island where the Aga Khan had a bungalow built for himself (his mausoleum stands on the western bank).

Further to the south the waters race through the locks of the dam, and behind the dam the Roman kiosk and the pylons that once graced Egypt's most beautiful sanctuaries can be seen reaching out of the reservoir. And behind this, Egypt's greatest modern building project is under way: the new dam whose waters will drive sixteen turbines that lie nearly 930 feet below the ground. A huge lake of twelve hundred square miles is being created, which will take four years to fill. Thus the landscape of Egypt is changing with the times: if Herodotus were to come to Egypt today or tomorrow he would scarcely recognize it.

FROM EGYPT'S HISTORY

A stairway is being built for him, so that he may ascend toward Heaven upon it.
(Pyramid inscription)

While Europe wallowed in the vast swamplands of the postglacial period, Egypt possessed a highly developed civilization of which very little is known. The history of Egypt begins around 5000 B.C. when a remarkable natural phenomenon occurred: large regions of the fertile plain dried up, turned into steppes, and later into sandy deserts. The people were driven toward the water, the Nile. They became acquainted with the floods and soon began to erect dams; they experienced lean years and constructed canals and storage basins to conserve water. And they have continued to do this till today. The origin of the Egyptian nation is lost in the unrecorded gray dawn of history; archeological excavations show that there were several different cultures. What we know of those distant days is that the new arrivals settled down as farmers, that they raised mainly cattle, sheep, goats, pigs, and dogs; that they buried their dead in the sand with faces turned to the west, and that they produced pottery.

They had to fight Libyan nomadic tribes who tried to crowd in from the west; they took possession of the regions bordering on the delta and pushed the southern boundary of their land up as far as Elephantine, the Aswân of today. The calendar was invented in Egypt as early as 4242 B.C., which proves the high level of their civilization. The kingdom was unified under Menes who brought both the "Northland" and the "Southland" under his scepter. With Menes we begin to count the dynasties, totaling thirty-one royal families, that ruled Egypt.

The Pyramid Builders

Southwest of Cairo, are the pyramids at the edge of the desert. There are dozens of them, structures of enormous size, dominating the plateau that reaches from Giza to Medum and the surrounding burial grounds. They all belong to the so-called "Pyramid Era" or "Old Kingdom." A tremendous spiritual upheaval must have preceded that period; for, if hitherto the king had been a world-god in close touch with the cosmos, there now was a superterrestrial god above him, a god who governs all becoming and being: the sun, giver of all life.

Zoser ruled around 2700 B.C. He had the first large-scale stone edifice built, the Step Pyramid of Saqqara, a structure of stones piled upon stones: six mastabas on top of one another.

Most tourists are content to visit the big Cheops pyramid and the pyramids of Chephren and Mycerinus. All three belong to the IVth dynasty.

Two million three hundred thousand stone blocks, each weighing two and a half tons, had to be dragged to the site and piled one above the other until the Cheops pyramid, that gigantic sacral structure, was completed. The work took twenty years. Each of its sides is 760 feet long; the pyramid is nearly 490 feet high. Its stones would fill five freight trains, each train as long as the distance from Vienna to Paris.

But how were these tremendous stones transported, since the quarries are nine miles away on the opposite bank of the Nile? How were they placed on top of each other? Historians rack their brains, construction engineers search for instruments and implements.

The problem begins with the question of blasting, since the Egyptians had no dynamite. And yet they performed the miracle of detaching large masses of stone from the rock – with nothing but wood and water at their disposal; perhaps they also used vinegar. Rows of holes were chiseled into the mountainside, wooden wedges were driven into the holes and then the wedges were made to swell by means of water. This process was repeated until the rock cracked.

From old Egyptian wall reliefs we know that the builders of that remote epoch transported blocks of granite on wooden sleds drawn by four ropes which were pulled by 172 workmen in rhythmic motion, probably accompanied by song. According to Herodotus, the pyramids were built in layers of stone which were placed one upon the other, each higher one being a step smaller than the one on which it rested. In his book this first great traveler into history reports that the Egyptians used short pieces of wood as levers to set block on block and that the over-all coating of the sides – of which today only a small portion at the tip of the Chephren pyramid remains – was applied from the top down. We know today that auxiliary ramps were used in the building of the pyramids. Over the centuries, voluminous works have been written about the meaning and purpose of the pyramids. Some explorers of the past believed that the pyramids were the "granaries of Joseph;" others had the fanciful idea that they might have served as bases for signal fires. An erroneous and misleading theory of mystical numbers was developed in connection with the pyramids, which is still alive today in astrology and other methods of "predicting the future." The Cheops pyramid served as burial place for the king and was the site of initiation into the ancient Egyptian mysteries.

Nor do we know very much about the period in which the pyramids were built. We do not even know exactly when the great Sphinx that towers above the Chephren temple below the Chephren pyramid came into being. The Sphinx measures sixty-six feet from the top of its head down to its front paws, and its over-all length is three hundred feet.

The Successors of the Pyramid Builders

The "Old Kingdom" fell victim to conflicting new philosophies. Not until 2040 B.C. did a king of the XIth dynasty, Mentuhotep, succeed in reuniting the divided country. A tightly controlled bureaucracy developed, but the vitality of the state diminished noticeably. The great irrigation systems and the draining of the Faiyûm basin, mentioned earlier, were the only great cultural achievements of that period.

Foreign Rule

Around the year 1650 B.C. a foreign shepherding people, the Hyksos, invaded Egypt from the north. They introduced the horse and battlewagon and ruled the country for 108 years. They were driven out by the princes of the XVIIth dynasty.

The New Kingdom

With the help of horses and carriages Egypt now became a politically and strategically powerful nation. And thus begins the glorious XVIIIth dynasty. Its story has the speed and excitement of a movie spectacular: the Kings Amenophis I and Thutmose I advanced as far as the Euphrates; Nubia was reconquered. Then a woman ascended the throne: Hatshepsut. She is one of the few remarkable figures in Egyptian history about whom much – though not everything – is known. She was married to her younger stepbrother,

Thutmose III, whom she completely overshadowed. In contrast to the expansionist tendencies of others of her dynasty, she reorganized the country from within and deliberately avoided wars; among her greatest achievements were the expeditions by sea to Punt and the construction of the terraced temple Deir el Bahari.

It is not known for certain whether Thutmose III killed her, but the fact remains that after her death Thutmose III had every trace of his spouse and rival erased. Soon afterward, the young king began military campaigns that resulted in Egypt's becoming a world power. During his reign the southern boundaries of Egypt were pushed as far as the fourth cataract of the Nile.

Ikhnaton

Soon after Thutmose III there emerged another king who showed but little interest in foreign conquests. He is one of the strangest figures in the history of the world. His name is Ikhnaton.

The more worldly the kingdom had become under his predecessors, Thutmose III and Amenophis III, the greater had been the efforts of the priests of Thebes to establish a theocracy. Ikhnaton attempted to free by force Egyptian civilization from the chains of tradition. For this reason he left the capital, Thebes, in the sixth year of his reign and founded Tell el 'Amarna, his City of the Sun, in Middle Egypt. He eradicated the worship of the old Theban gods and replaced them with Aten, the "living solar disk." His wife was the beautiful Nefertiti.

However, the Theban priests, realizing that this development meant loss of power for them, opposed the king's ideas; besides, Egypt began to topple from its position of world supremacy during Ikhnaton's reign. It is assumed that the "first herald of Christ," as Ikhnaton is sometimes called today, was put out of the way. For a while, his son-in-law, Tutankhamen, ruled under the tutelage of the generals of the army. Thebes again became the capital of the country and Tell el 'Amarna fell to ruin.

The Ramessides

Under Seti I, founder of the XIXth dynasty, the country recovered. He was only one of the Pharaohs who led Egypt back to the pinnacle of political and spiritual power. Like his predecessors and successors, he built temples throughout the country. The stone monuments at Luxor proclaim his deeds.

Great upheavals took place in the Near East during the time of Seti. The ancient Bronze Age peoples were replaced by new nations whose power was based on their use of iron. Tribes from the north overran the Hittite and Mitanni kingdoms, others followed them to the sea. They subjugated all of Anatolia, swept over Syria, probably captured Crete, and attacked the western delta in Egypt. Another wave of migrating tribes destroyed Palestine and invaded Egypt by way of the Sinai mountains.

They were halted in their progress by Ramses III. He destroyed his enemies in great battles on land and sea; survivors were mutilated. Terrible are the scenes that were chiseled into the temple walls of Medinet Habu by the Pharaoh's stone masons.

These wars weakened Egypt's economy considerably. But it is significant for that period that the Ramesside kings returned to the ancient spiritual and religious ideas and dogmas and that their temples, from the delta up to Abu Simbel, were decorated in the most lavish way. Gradually, the spiritual content of the old religion was lost in a materialistic world view. Where, in the Old Kingdom, up to the time of Ikhnaton, all concepts of life and after-life had been fraught with deep, spiritual meaning, there now appeared decadence, which was bound to lead toward a general decline. The ancient mysteries were lost; the belief in animal gods – still meaningful during the Old Kingdom – took on an incomprehensible form; the embalming of the dead was practiced only in memory of an older cult; it had become a business proposition. Art suffered a change, too. Under Ramses I and Ramses II the scenes cut into the temple walls lost their character; mass production of stereotyped arts and crafts developed. Even in the chambers of the dead, mundane matters became prominent: among other things, we find wild scenes of orgies and debauchery from the dead man's life which also confirm the impression of a general decline.

The Late Period

In the course of time, Egypt was conquered by the Ethiopians and Assyrians. In the time of the XXVIth dynasty Greek culture found its way into the country, and Saïs, in the delta, became the capital and the most important trade center in the north.

Around 525 B.C., Cambyses conquered Egypt and reduced it to a Persian province. Thus began a rapid deterioration of what was still left of Egypt's ancient, if degenerating, civilization. When Alexander the Great reached the Nile in 332 B.C., Egypt's power had waned. Not even Cleopatra, a clever and energetic queen (69-30 B.C.) was able to save its sinking star. She had a love affair with Julius Caesar, bore him a son, then traveled to Rome, where she led a life of ease in her lover's gardens. After Caesar's assassination she hurried back to Egypt. She was called to account by Antony in the year 41, after which she became his mistress and led a life of unparalleled hedonism. Both committed suicide.

Romans and Christians

Christianity came early to the land of the Pharaohs, while the Romans ruled the country. Monasticism and anchoritism developed. But in the third century there began a time of bloody persecution of Christians and great suffering that did not end until the reign of Constantine the Great (A.D. 324-337). About fifty years later, Theodosius I established Christianity as the official state religion. The first Coptic translations of the Bible date from that period.

Islam

Roman domination was followed by the Byzantine period (395-640). In about 450 the Egyptian Coptic Church was founded. But soon after the death of Mohammed (632) his successor, Omar I, invaded Egypt, which now fell into the hands of the Arabs. Thus the land on the Nile became an Islamic country.

The oldest Islamic university in the world, the Mosque El Azhar, founded in 978 made Cairo (*al Qâhira* – "The Victorious") the spiritual center of the entire Arab world,

In 1218 the first crusaders set foot on Egyptian soil; then, from the middle of the thirteenth century until the end of the Middle Ages, Egypt was under the rule of the Mamelukes.

Napoleon

Napoleon's Egyptian campaign in 1798 was of enormous importance for historical and cultural research. For, had Napoleon gone to Turkey instead, it is unlikely that a certain stone, polished and covered with inscriptions on one side, would ever have been found. An unknown French soldier picked it up near Rosetta, in the delta – and, since Napoleon had brought along a whole regiment of first-rate scientists, that stone received the attention it deserved.

As it turned out, the inscriptions were in hieroglyphs as well as in demotic and Greek characters. The Greek part of the inscription could be read. Its content was a dedication by the priests of Memphis honoring Ptolemy V (*c.* 196 B.C.). The other characters, the hieroglyphs which no one had been able to understand until then, were deciphered after long and arduous study by Jean-François Champollion, who thus became the founder of Egyptology.

Mehemet Ali

There is yet another name intimately connected with the destiny of Egypt: Mehemet Ali, an Albanian who could neither read nor write. He is considered the founder of modern Egypt and of a dynasty that began in 1805 and ended in 1952. He "defeated" the Mameluke beys by giving a big party in their honor at his citadel and massacring his unsuspecting guests – 480 beys in all. Afterward he did much to benefit his country. He directed the permanent irrigation and regulation of the waters in the Nile delta, imported cotton, and had large industrial plants built. A farsighted ruler, he also called in Frenchmen, Englishmen, and Germans who helped in the country's development.

After his death in 1849, his successors quickly led the country down the road to destruction. His heritage was squandered. Abbas I turned out to be a foe of all things European; crisis followed crisis. Twenty years later the Suez Canal was opened with a great deal of ceremony, but the country was at the point of bankruptcy. England was able to buy a large portion of the Suez Canal shares, thus securing for herself control over this important waterway. In 1882, after some clashes between Europeans and an Egyptian mob in Alexandria, England occupied the country. The protectorate was not lifted until 1922, when Egypt became an independent state once more.

The End of the Monarchy

On the night of July 22, 1952, a military junta intervened in the country's destiny. In a coup d'état King Farouk, accused of corruption, was deposed and banished from the country. For a while, the former Major General Mohammed Naguib headed a revolutionary committee; later he was elected President and Premier and the monarchy, which by then existed on paper only, was officially repealed. A few months later, on February 25, 1954, Naguib was ousted by Gamal Abdel Nasser. That day the people of Cairo cheered their new President of the Revolution and Premier, Nasser – and another chapter in Egypt's history began.

CIVILIZATION OF THE ANCIENT EGYPTIANS

The Calendar

The ancient Egyptians invented the calendar. They introduced it around the year 4242 B.C. They based it on observations concerning the annual flooding of the Nile. The farmer's year began when the star Sothis first appeared at dawn on the Egyptian horizon.

There was a time span of $365\frac{1}{4}$ days between its initial appearances.

The Art of Writing

Herodotus quotes the Egyptians as calling themselves the oldest civilization on earth.

The walls of temples and the interiors of some pyramids of the Vth dynasty, tombs, obelisks, and columns and many statuettes given to the dead are covered with hieroglyphs. The best hieroglyphic writing can be found on wooden tablets, limestone walls, and papyri. Papyrus is a plant no longer found growing wild in Egypt, but in earlier times it covered large areas of the country. The plant was cut into strips of even thickness which were placed parallel to each other; a second layer was placed on top with the strips running at right angles to the layer beneath. The layers were pressed to form a sheet of even thickness.

The papyri that have come down to us speak a multiple language. They contain philosophy, aphorisms, prophecies; they describe the court trials of grave robbers; they describe magic tricks. We find tales, shepherd's stories, laments, songs, and charming folk tales that show us how lovingly the ancient Egyptians observed plant and animal life.

Dynasty

We know that in the government offices of ancient Egypt lists of all former kings were kept. These lists contained the name of each king and the length of his reign; they were also divided into groups.

This division into groups was made by the Egyptians themselves. In the Turin Papyrus the list of kings is divided into periods and the years of rule are tabulated for each period. The arrangement by dynasties is attributed to Manetho, who was high priest in Heliopolis under King Ptolemy I. He divided the reigns from Menes to Darius into thirty-one dynasties or ruling houses. This arrangement has been retained for practical reasons, although the grouping does not always correspond with the actual genealogy.

About the Gods

The god *Amen* or *Amon* was the chief deity of Thebes. The jackal-headed *Anubis* was the divine protector of the dead. In Memphis, the sacred bull *Apis* was worshiped. Ikhnaton worshiped the divine disk of the sun, who became *Aten*, the reigning deity in the royal capital of Amarna. *Atum* was the sun god in the priest city of Heliopolis. The cat was considered a sacred animal and was worshiped as *Bast*, goddess of joy. The sun god in the form of a scarab was named *Khepera*, while the ram-headed god, *Khnemu*, presided over the cataracts. *Herakhti* was a special form of the sun god *Horus* and was worshiped in the form of a falcon. *Horus* was the sun god, son of Isis and Osiris. In the sky resided the goddess *Hathor*, "Cow of Heaven." *Isis* was the mother goddess. *Osiris*, her husband, was the god of the dead and in Abydos he was "Lord of the western people." He was both judge and ruler in the realm of the dead. *Geb* was an earth god, husband of *Nut*, goddess of the heavens, frequently depicted with star-studded body. The goddess of order and justice was *Maat*, who wore an ostrich plume on her head as symbol of her dignity. The god of fertility was *Min*, recognizable on temple wall paintings by his erect member.

Protector of artists and sculptors was the god *Ptah*, who was also the chief god of Memphis, capital of the Old Kingdom.

Ra was another name of the sun god. He traveled across the eastern sky in the barge of the morning and traversed the western sky in the barge of the evening.

Temples and Obelisks

The temples of the Old Kingdom were made of brick and have not come down to us.

Only the burial temples of the kings, the pyramids and sun temples of the third to the sixth dynasties were made of stone. The burial temple of a king was originally a place of sacrifice near the tomb. Some experts believe that it consisted of a small-scale model of the royal palace some distance from the grave, in which the spirit of the king was supposed to continue to live.

Researchers in the field of religion tell us that the obelisk represents the ray of the sun. Processional roads flanked by sphinxes sometimes led from one temple site to another. One such avenue of rams and sphinxes still exists at Karnak (see picture 59).

The Tombs of the Kings

The oldest royal tombs are not pyramids. The kings of the first and second dynasties repose near Abydos in simple rectangular chambers which later were enlarged and had storage rooms added to them.

The development of the pyramid begins with the IIIrd dynasty. This kind of entombment was used, in somewhat altered form, until the New Kingdom. Thutmose is believed to have been the first ruler who had his tomb placed in the Valley of the Kings. These tombs contain chambers, labyrinths, and trap doors designed to keep out undesirable invaders. They descend as far as three hundred feet and are as long as 703 feet. Some corridors and halls have remained unexplored to this day. The only well-preserved and but slightly plundered tomb that has been discovered is that of Tutankhamen.

Most of the royal tombs were robbed in the time of the Pharaohs. We know this from existing papyri on which the court trials of apprehended grave robbers are recorded. Such mummies of kings and Pharaohs as have been preserved now repose in a number of museums. In the Archaeological Museum in Cairo they are kept in a special room where they can be viewed upon special request.

Similarly, the treasures that have been found in the various tombs have been distributed among museums all over the world. The most important collection is in Cairo, where not nearly everything that has been found can be put on view. A new museum is being planned.

Priests, Soldiers, and Other Human Figures

The priests were always depicted in a short apron, the priests of Sem in a panther skin; the priestly readers wore a sash across the chest. Workers and members of the lower classes were usually dressed with a cloth around the belt; children went naked and soldiers wore a triangular cloth at the front of their short apron.

The oldest Egyptians are shown with long hair and pointed beards. At the beginning of recorded history men wore their hair short and their faces were clean-shaven. Later, wigs were worn: short ones with curls or long ones with straight hair. The women of the Old Kingdom had wigs reaching down to their shoulders. There are pictures that show both men and women with shaven heads. Dancing girls wore their hair in a long braid weighted by a ball, or they wore their hair short.

Clothing was varied. We find loincloths or plaited aprons. A short tunic of linen seems to have been common. The man's tunic was white. Women wore long, tight-fitting shifts held up by shoulder straps. In the New Kingdom women usually wore slim shifts that left the right shoulder bare. Over this they sometimes wore a coat that was knotted across the breast.

Games and Sport

Many paintings depict games. There was a popular board game similar to chess. A game that young people still like to play, especially in Italy, was known to the Egyptians: guessing a number by means of suddenly outstretched fingers.

Jumping and leapfrog can be recognized in many pictures. Ballgames, too, were popular with Egyptians in all walks of life. In the houses, many of which were sumptuously appointed with elegant furniture, music was often performed. Hand clapping accompanied the playing of flute or tambourine. Dancing girls showed their skill. Many fashionable households employed blind harpists. Some harpist's songs of unforgettable beauty have come down to us from that period.

ABOUT THE LAND

They tremble who see the Nile when it flows. The fields laugh, the banks are flooded. The sacrifices of the god descend, the faces of men are bright, and the hearts of the gods rejoice.

(From an ancient poem)

Geography

Egypt can be compared to a nut: the two halves of the shell are the rocky mountain range bordering on the Sahara, covered with shifting golden sands and, in the east, the alternately slate-gray and red-glowing Arabian Desert. The meat of the nut is the fertile strip of land, half a mile to sixty miles wide and 751 miles long, reaching from Aswân to the mouth of the delta and composed of water, silt, and earth deposited in the course of thousands of years.

Egypt covers an area of 384,000 square miles of which ninety-seven per cent is desert, sand, stone, steppe. The remaining three per cent of fertile land must feed thirty million people. The western border runs south from the Gulf of Sollum; to the east, the Red Sea forms a natural border; the southern boundary of the country is at Adindan (near the twenty-second parallel).

Since time immemorial Egypt has been divided into two halves: Lower Egypt in the north and Upper Egypt in the south. The delta, which measures seven thousand square miles and includes Cairo, is part of Lower Egypt and contains nine provinces, including the Suez Canal and Port Saïd. The eight provinces of Upper Egypt lie to the south of Cairo; their border begins between Giza and Saqqara. The region reaches as far as Aswân, where there

begins yet a third region which, in a few years, will be known as the "water reservoir."

In speaking of Egypt's fertile regions we must not forget the oases. They are all located on the western bank of the Nile, separated from the river by stretches of desert. Their names are Siwa, El Khârga, El Bahariya, El Farafra, and El Dakhla.

The population of the western oases is isolated from the Nile valley by large valleys which are partly below sea level, and by stretches of desert. Natural wells and many artificial ones help keep the soil fertile. Not far from the oases we find great wandering sand dunes and then the huge sand sea – regions that have remained partially unexplored.

On the eastern bank of the Nile there are roads and pathways leading, sometimes through precipitous gorges, to the Red Sea, where mountain ranges reach an elevation of six thousand feet. This area is almost completely arid. So is the Sinai Peninsula, whose mountains also reach a height of six thousand feet.

Climate

There is little rainfall in Egypt. Cairo has an average of five to seven days of rain a year. Only Alexandria and the coastal regions have rain during the winter months of November through February. In winter, the temperature rarely goes below 32° F. Days are warm and dry. In summer the temperature can go as high as 126° F., especially around Luxor and Aswân. The temperature differential between day and night is 50 to 65 degrees.

Average temperatures	Dec.-Jan.	Jul.-Aug.
Alexandria	57° F.	79°-80° F.
Cairo	56° F.	83°-84° F.
Aswân	62° F.	92°-104° F.

During the months of December to April there are sometimes sand storms that move the western rim of the desert toward the Nile. They bring with them a hot wind that has an enervating effect.

Geology

The Libyan Desert consists of a limestone plateau. Fossils of shellfish are still being found in great numbers on the plateau near Thebes. Fine yellow sand blows continually across this region but sand dunes appear only in the Aswân region. On this completely barren plateau phosphates and alum can be found and, in some places, sodium. The Arabian Desert, on the eastern shore of the Nile, is made up of crystalline rock. Granite, diorite, hornblende, and gneiss are found there. Among other minerals are manganese, iron, talc, asbestos, gold, basalt, and red granite. Limestone and sandstone form a large plateau near Cairo and further to the south. Numerous fossils, including a petrified forest, can be found around Cairo.

Irrigation

Every year in midsummer the waters of the Nile overflow their banks. The flood fertilizes the land. (As soon as the waters recede, the fellahin supplement the irrigation of their fields along the canals, using ancient methods of drawing up water.)

According to a UNESCO report it has been calculated that in August and September 175 billion cubic feet of water are lost between Aswân and Asyût, and that between Asyût and Cairo about 3,530 cubic feet are lost every second. These quantities are negligible compared to the Nile floods which reach a volume of nearly 320,000 cubic feet per second during that season. Yet, the year-round average amount of water in the river comes to only 76,630 cubic feet per second.

The construction of a new reservoir above Aswân will turn about 1,150 square miles of desert into an inland lake and reclaim about two and a half million acres of desert land for agriculture. Six hundred fifty thousand acres which are now under water will be drained. The wall of the new dam, Sadd El Aali, will be 230 feet high and three miles long. It will create an artificial lake 290 miles in length and with a capacity of nearly 460 billion cubic feet. The dam becomes a vital necessity for Egypt, whose population is expected to increase by about eight million within the next ten years.

Plants and Animals

There are no forests in Egypt, unless one considers the palm oases as such.

Ancient Egypt had vast grazing lands where cattle was raised. Today the country is planted mainly with sugar cane, cotton, grain, cattle feed, and orchards.

During March and April the desert blooms in those regions where rainfall occurs.

Date and doom palms grow along the Nile and in the oases; there also are olives, lemons bananas, tangerines, mangoes, figs, grapes, pomegranates, peaches, and apricots. Decorative plants include carnations, oleander, roses, and mallows. Of legumes, there are beans, lentils, peas, lupines; of grains: wheat, corn, rice, barley. Fodder, clover, rapeseed, and mustard grow over wide areas. Onions are exported; pumpkins, cucumbers, tomatoes, garlic, radishes, and beets are grown, as well as a kind of wild parsley. Among the chief agricultural products are cotton and cane sugar.

In ancient Egypt there were lions, hippopotamuses, ichneumons, crocodiles, giraffes, and ostriches. These animals exist only in zoos nowadays. On the other hand, there still exists an abundance of jackals, scarabs, cows, cats, dogs, camels, donkeys, fine Arabian horses, pigeons, geese, ducks, sheep, goats, and dark-skinned water buffaloes. The white cow-heron is protected by the farmers because it eats the insects that plague the cattle. The Nile is rich in fish. Countless wading birds dwell in the swamplands.

Population

Egypt is known as a melting pot for a variety of nationalities. Seventy-five to eighty per cent of all the country's inhabitants are *fellahin*, meaning farmers; seven to eight per cent are Coptic Christians. The rest of the population is composed of Bedouins, Nubians, Negroes, Persians, Indians, Syrians, Armenians, Turks, Lebanese, Jews, and Europeans. According to the last census in 1957, there were at that time 2,000 North Americans, 1,573 Germans, 1,400 Swiss, 445 Austrians, and citizens of various other countries in Egypt. Many have since left the country. Not included in this census are the experts from Russia and other countries working on various projects, including the big dam.

Economy

In the past few years the population's income, which had been very low, has somewhat improved. But the figures from the years 1949 and 1959 are mostly out of date and even the 1961 results can no longer be considered entirely valid.

The only possible way for Egypt to strengthen her economy is to industrialize and expand her agrarian production (which in turn depends on the water supply). The strongest industry is the textile industry; next come the food industry, metal products, chemicals, cotton ginning, tobacco, oil, and electricity. Most of Egypt's industry is concentrated around Cairo and Alexandria. It employs about 400,000 people. Egypt has introduced a form of planned economy called "Arab Socialism."

Culture

Scarcely another country in the world consumes the doubtful products of radio and motion pictures in such quantities – not to say to such excess – as does Egypt. However, especially in Cairo and Alexandria, literature, painting, and music also flourish. In recent years a number of literary works of Egyptian origin have been translated into foreign lan-

22

guages. Egyptian music tends to be oriental in flavor and is designed to cater to the popular taste, but recently the works of European masters have found favor with the Egyptians. Verdi, whose popularity dates back to the monarchy and to Aïda, which he composed in honor of the opening of the Suez Canal, still enjoys a great vogue in Egypt.

Ninety-one per cent of Egyptians are Muslim. The Copts are still holding their own, and most of the other Christian churches are represented in Egypt.

Despite a marked tendency toward Europeanization and Americanization, the country is striving for independence and is trying with every means at its disposal to preserve its national identity.

Translated by Maria Pelikan

Captions in fold-out at the end of the book

4

Mayest thou protect the living hawk, the son of Ra, the eternal, the beloved of Ptah, with this papyrus stalk in thy hand in this thy name.   (From a prayer)

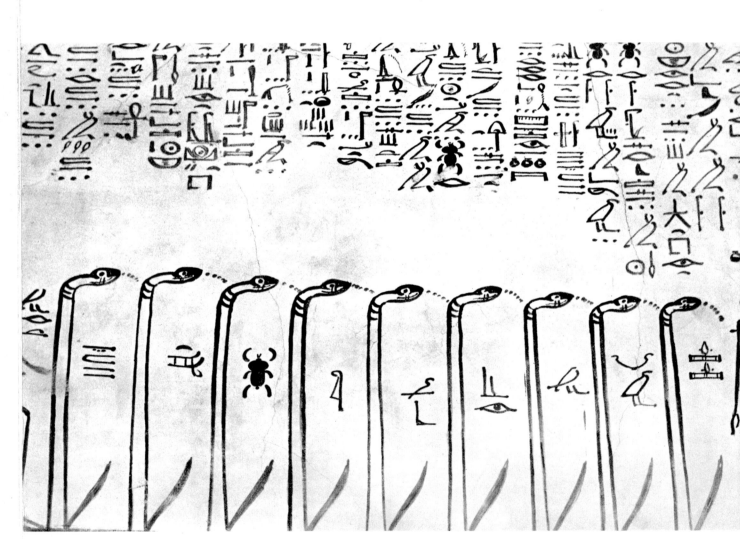

51

50

How splendid is thy emergence at the edge of the sky,
O living Aten, giver of life!
When thou appearest in the eastern sky,
Thou fillest that land with thy beauty.
Thou art kind and great, thy brilliance stands high above all the land.
Thy rays embrace the lands, as far as thy creation reaches.
Though thou be far away, thy rays strike the earth;
And the faces of men are thy mirror.

The earth brightens when thou arisest at the edge of the sky
And appearest as Aten by day.
Thou drivest away the darkness as soon as thou givest us thy rays.
Then Egypt sparkles in festive raiment.
Men awake and arise;
For thou hast called them up.
They wash their limbs and reach for their clothes.
At the sight of thee, they raise their arms in adoration.
And then the whole country goes to work.

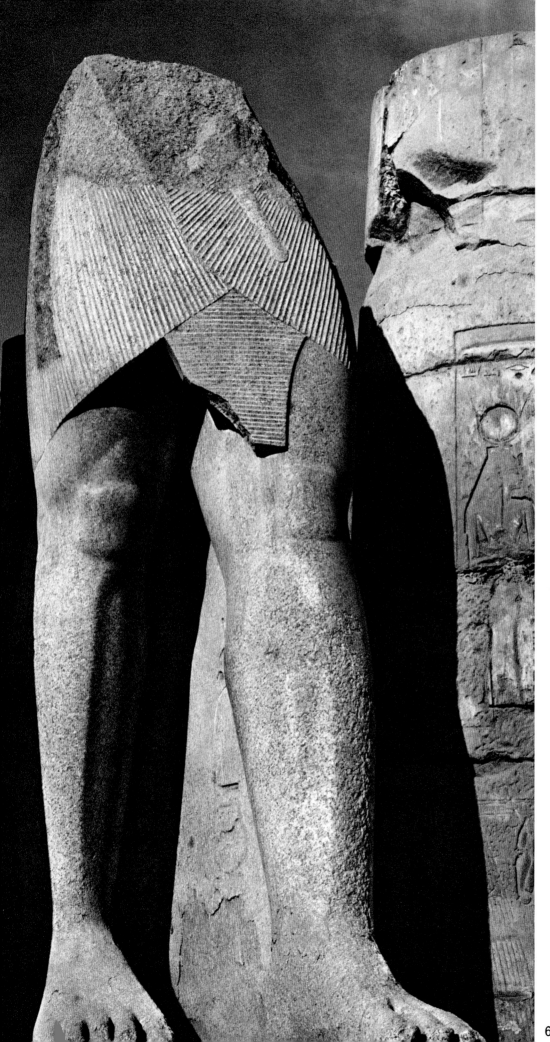

72

sun. Rare rains transform wide stretches of this desert into a carpet of flowers.

25. The pyramid near Saqqara (also called the Step Pyramid) was built under King Zoser. It is the first great stone structure – a memorial edifice composed of six mastabas placed atop one another.

26. Veiled women, carrying water pitchers on their heads, walk home along the edge of the desert.

27. An entirely different kind of people live in the Siwa Oasis, which Alexander the Great once visited.

28. In the early morning hours the fellahin take their camels to the fields to harvest grain.

29. Monks still live in the St. Catherine monastery in the Sinai Peninsula. The monastery has a library of about eight thousand manuscripts, among which are copies of the Old Testament.

30. View of the St. Catherine monastery. Cypresses grow in the beautiful cloister garden.

31. Fellahin at their threshing. The threshing cart is drawn by domestic animals.

32. Aerial photograph of threshing operations in the delta. The grain harvest takes place when it is spring in North America.

33. This is the way the desert looks on the Libyan side as seen from an airplane. There are valleys and small mountain ranges up to six hundred feet in height.

34. A young Egyptian from a fellah village.

35. In the oasis of El Kharga some ancient customs dating back to the Pharaohs are still in force. The Romans and early Christians constructed imposing buildings here. Two temples of the Emperor Hadrian still stand. Our picture shows a mosque.

36. Women carrying water is not a rare sight in Egypt.

37. Ikhnaton abandoned Thebes and the old gods in order to build a sun city in Tell el 'Amarna. But Ihknaton's successors destroyed many of the rock tombs containing magnificent paintings.

38. In the Temple of Deir el-Bahri: the Queen Hatshepsut imbibing life from the cow Hathor.

39. One of the masterpieces in the ruins of Karnak: A granite pillar with lotus flowers, a work of the XVIIIth Dynasty.

40. View across the entrance hall of the Temple Medinet Habu in the necropolis of Thebes. On the exterior wall, a representation of the naval battle against the people from the north. From the reign of Ramses III.

41. The photograph shows an unfinished relief from the time of Ikhnaton at Tell el 'Amarna. Many of the twenty-five rock tombs were never finished.

42. The prehistoric kings of the Ist and IInd Dynasties used Abydos as a burial place. Tha Seti Temple – its roof supported by gigantic columns – dates from the New Kingdom.

43 and 44. Hathor is believed to have been the goddess of the dead in Deir el-Bahri. She was not only depicted in the form of a cow, but also standing on columns, wearing a sistrum. These columns are in the upper part of the Hatshepsut Terrace-Temple in Deir el-Bahri. Behind the mountain range lies the Valley of the Kings.

45. One of the numerous Pharaoh tombs in the Valley of the Kings (Thebes). The galleries descend as deep as five hundred feet into the rock, but this did not prevent grave robbers from entering, plundering, and opening the sarcophagi. Tutankhamen's tomb, however was untouched.

46. All the pictures in the private and royal tombs in the Thebes area (just west of Luxor) stem from the New Kingdom. A painting from the tomb of Userhet in Thebes.

47. The sacrifice bearer in the grave of Ramose (XVIIIth Dynasty, Thebes) carries three papyrus stalks with open blossoms. These artful representations have much in common with those found at Tell el 'Amarna. In the burial field at Thebes they are unique.

48. Hieroglyphs in rose-colored granite in the ruins of Karnak.

49. A scene from the frieze of the funeral procession in the tomb of Ramose at Thebes, depicting bearers of sacrificial offerings and lamenting women.

50. A lady and her servant from the tomb of Zesekeresonb at Thebes. An unusually beautiful wall painting.

51. In the tombs of the Ramessides in the Valley of the Kings we find pictures resembling those found in the papyrus of the Book of the Dead, such as this snake frieze.

52. A group of musicians from the XVIIIth Dynasty in the tomb of Nakht in Thebes.

53. Ikhnaton worshiped the sun as the god Aten. The representation of the solar disk shows rays which end in hands that give and bless.

54. Painting from the tomb of Rekhmire at Thebes. These interesting scenes show laborers at work.

55. From "Thebes of the Hundred Doors." Huge doors closed the temple entrances. Photographed at Karnak.

56. High relief from the tomb of Ramose at Thebes.

57. The largest and most impressive temple sites of ancient Egypt are in Luxor and Karnak. At left, in the sunlight, the sphinxlike head of a king.

58. Detail of the avenue of rams and sphinxes near Karnak.

59. The great avenue of sphinxes in front of the temple of Karnak.

60. The obelisks of Karnak were meant to remind man of his inherent powers for good. They are more than sixty-five feet high.

61. A fellah woman carrying water from the Nile near Aswân.

62. In the quarries near Aswân there is a granite obelisk which has been only partially removed from the rock. These colossal stones were taken from the rock in one piece by means of water or vinegar: the liquid was poured into specially drilled holes into which wooden wedges had been driven.

63. The Pharaoh between two godesses. From the Temple of Kom Ombo in Upper Egypt.

64. The tips of the obelisks, which symbolize the rays of the sun, were covered with gold leaf. The sides are inscribed with hieroglyphs.

65. A school in the Dakhla Oasis. In recent years Egypt has begun to promote general education.

66. Head of the divine Horus falcon from the temple at Idfu.

67. Idfu. The temple walls are completely covered with hieroglyphs and scenes from the life of the king.

68. Many of the colossal granite statues of the Pharaohs in the temples of Luxor and Karnak have come down to us only as fragments.

69. One of the most beautiful temple colonnades of ancient Egypt, built under Amenophis III at Luxor. It is 148.5 feet long and 168 feet wide.

70. Nubian boatman on the Nile.

71. Barges sailing along the Nile toward sundown are a picturesque sight. Shown here: a felucca.

72. In the Luxor and Aswân regions large rocks are transported by ship. They are used to reinforce the river bed, because the Nile can rise up to thirty feet and badly damage the dam.

73. The dam at Aswân is 168 feet high; its construction was originally begun in 1898. The wall is ninety-nine feet thick at the base and has 180 sluice gates through which the water is distributed.

74. Possibly the most beautiful temples in Egypt lie behind the dam in the basin of the artificial lake. They are the sanctuaries of Philae; they emerge from the water during a few months every year only.

75. The Nubian desert is rocky and bare. Photograph shows a cemetery with tombs made of silt from the Nile.

76. Entrance to a typical Nubian house. The wooden door is painted with colored designs.

77. A fellah woman in front of her dwelling. The house is built of bricks made of silt from the Nile.

78. At the camel market in Aswân.

79. In the old days, Mohammedans who had made the pilgrimage to Mecca recorded their journey to the holy city by painting their means of transportation on the walls of their houses. In many places, however, these paintings have lost their original meaning and have become mere ornaments.

80. A branch of the Nile in Upper Egypt.

81. Ramses II built the sanctuary of Abu Simbel and dedicated it to the gods Amon Ra of Thebes and Herakhti of Heliopolis. Each of the four seated Pharaohs is sixty-six feet high. The statues are hewn from the rock. There is a plan to lift the temple with the aid of UNESCO; if not lifted, the temple will disappear in the new reservoir.

82. Detail from the colossal statues of Ramses II at Abu Simbel.

83. The Nile near Aniba, Nubia. Aniba is in the region of the new reservoir, north of Abu Simbel.

84. The second, smaller temple at Abu Simbel was dedicated by Ramses II to his wife Nefertari, and to the goddess Hathor.

85 and 86. In the rock temple of Abu Simbel, whose overall length is 180 feet, pillars depicting the king support the hall, which measures fifty-six feet by fifty-two feet.

87. Nefertari, the wife of Ramses II. This is one of the numerous statues at Abu Simbel. Both temples are built to face east.

Back Cover: In the foreground, the silhouette of the Chephren pyramid near Giza; in the background the Cheops pyramid. The latter is considered the most perfect of these burial edifices.

PICTURE CAPTIONS

Picture Captions

Cover: A woman from the El Kharga oasis, carrying a water pitcher.

1. When tourist ships steam along the banks of the Nile in Upper Egypt, they get a rousing welcome from the youngsters.
2. An ocean of sand surrounds the oases of the Libyan Desert. Strong winds often drive the wandering dunes close to the palm groves.
3. The face of this young Egyptian woman from Luxor calls to mind the faces depicted on the walls of many a burial chamber dating back to the time of the Pharaohs.
4. These conical towers are inhabited by pigeons; about two thousand birds live in each such cove. They yield about fifty 45-pound bags of fertilizer a year. Each bag is worth seven to eight dollars. During the winter months the pigeons are fed maize, rice, and beans. The rest of the year they find their own food.
5. Once a week is market day in Luxor. There you can see figures in long robes straight out of the Bible. Every pot and dish is haggled over in true oriental style.
6. The mosques of Cairo are near the Citadel and Khan el Khalil (bazaar). The mosque of Ibn-Tulun was built around A.D. 876 on the hill of Qal-at-el-Kebsh by Ahmed Ibn Tulun; the fountain resembles a sheik's tomb.
7. In the domed interior of the Alabaster Mosque of Mohammed Ali (the Citadel), beautifully tinted windows and impressive lamps create fascinating light effects.
8. Friday prayers in the mosque. The faithful, who are not allowed to touch the floor with their shoes, prostrate themselves on straw mats, then bow toward Mecca, the holy city of Islam.
9. There are comparatively few objects that have been discovered dating back to the Ist Dynasty. This wooden statue is from the IIIrd or IVth Dynasty. It was found at Saqqara, the necropolis near Memphis.
10. Tutankhamen's death mask was found in the Valley of the Kings. A great example of the goldsmith's art, the mask is inlaid with crystal, vitreous paste, and lapis lazuli. (Cairo Museum.)
11. Night life in Cairo.
12. Cairo at night. The modern buildings are bathed in the light of neon signs. Ten years ago, this street consisted of hovels.
13. The Dakhla Oasis, a day's trip to the west of El Kharga, is completely surrounded by the wasteland of the Libyan Desert. This oasis is among the most beautiful spots in Egypt. The houses are made of dried mud.
14. In the streets of Cairo. Carrying their produce into the capital on donkey's back, the country folk pay scant attention to modern trucks and buses.
15. The *shadoof* (water scoop), which dates back to Biblical times, is still used by Egyptians to raise water from wells and canals into the fields.
16. Egyptian woman from Asyût, where a wolf-headed war god was worshiped. Asyût today is the largest city (population 100,000) in the province bearing the same name (population 1,500,000).
17. The great Sphinx at Giza dates back to the Old Kingdom. The human head rests on a lion's body hewn from rock. The Sphinx is three hundred feet long and sixty-six feet high. It is uncertain whether she was built under Chephren, Cheops, or a still earlier king. Her nose was damaged by cannon balls when the Mamelukes, in the time of Napoleon, used her as a target.
18. The ear of the Sphinx is four and a half feet high, the mouth measures 7.6 feet, and the face 13.7 feet. The nose was 5.6 feet long.
19. Aerial photograph of the three great pyramids at Giza. The Cheops pyramid, in the foreground, can be climbed. Its original height was 483.8 feet. Its base is 750.7 feet. Behind it are the pyramids of Chephren (originally 473.5 feet high) and Mycerinus (originally 219.4 feet high). Other, smaller pyramids are seen in its background. The picture clearly shows the present entrance into the Cheops pyramid.
20 and 21. Silhouettes since time immemorial. The pyramids of Giza on the western plateau, at the edge of the Libyan Desert.
22. If you want to reach the oases you have to put up with this kind of desert trail.
23. Near the monastery of St. Catherine, on the Sinai Peninsula, you may still come upon nomads whose wives veil their faces in the old manner.
24. The Sinai Desert is rocky. Caravans of seemingly endless length traverse it in the hot glare of the

ABOUT THE PHOTOGRAPHY:

Hed Wimmer uses the Rolleiflex and the Rolleicord. Adox 17 film was used throughout.

HED WIMMER, born August 3, 1920, began her professional career as a librarian. From 1952 to 1954 she studied at the Bavarian State School for Photography. Her travels first took her to Provence and Libya, Tunisia, Algeria, and Morocco. In 1957 she went to Egypt, in 1958 once

PLEASE FOLD OUT ▶

Picture 6 is from the book *Le Nil* published by Editions Clairefontaine.

CHRONOLOGICAL OUTLINE OF ANCIENT EGYPTIAN HISTORY

Prehistoric period:
Neolithic and Aëneolithic period
4242 – Egyptians invent the calendar.

5000–2900 B.C.

Archaic Period: Ist–IInd Dynasties
The kingdom is united under Menes.

2900–2600 B.C.

Old Kingdom: IIIrd–VIth Dynasties
Step pyramids. The great pyramid builders Cheops, Chephren, Mycerinus. Sun worship becomes the official religion. Mastabas near Saqqara with artistic representations of the life of the period. Attempts at restoration of the kingdom. Collapse.

2600–2190 B.C.

First Intermediate Period: VIIth–Xth Dynasties
Civil war between two royal houses.

2190–2040 B.C.

Middle Kingdom: XIth–XIVth Dynasties
Unification under local princes from Upper Egypt. A period of splendor under Amenemhet and Sesostris. Egypt's borders extend from Syria to Nubia. Drainage projects in Faiyûm.

2040–1710 B.C.

Second Intermediate Period: XVth–XVIth Dynasties (Hyksos)
Foreign "shepherd kings" rule Egypt. A capital is founded in the delta. The horse is introduced into the country. Upper Egypt ruled by various petty kings.

1710–1580 B.C.

New Kingdom: XVIIth–XXth Dynasties
The Hyksos are expelled. Hatshepsut sends an expedition to Punt. The golden age of Egyptian civilization. Egypt becomes a world power and is in close contact with the civilization of western Asia. Amarna period under Ikhnaton. "One god: Aten." Nefertiti. The Ramessides (Ramses III–XI). Cities and temples are built. War against the "Northern or Sea peoples." Return to the ancient dogmas and religious concepts.

1580–1085 B.C.

Period of Decline: XXIst–XXIVth Dynasties
Reign of the priests of Amen. Libyan soldier kings rule Egypt.

1085–715 B.C.

Late Period: XXVth–XXXIst Dynasties
Ethiopians and Assyrians struggle for the kingdom. Persian rule. Local princes expel the foreign kings. Second Persian reign.

715–332 B.C.

Greek Period:
Alexander the Great and the Ptolemies.

332–30 B.C.

Roman Period:

30 B.C.–A.D. 395